The dog-tax, a poem. By Edward Nairne, of Sandwich, in Kent. Including a hint to the minister for the relief of dogs, and the improvement of the revenue.

Edward Nairne

ECCO
PRINT EDITIONS

Eighteenth Century
Collections Online
Print Editions

Gale ECCO Print Editions

Relive history with *Eighteenth Century Collections Online*, now available in print for the independent historian and collector. This series includes the most significant English-language and foreign-language works printed in Great Britain during the eighteenth century, and is organized in seven different subject areas including literature and language; medicine, science, and technology; and religion and philosophy. The collection also includes thousands of important works from the Americas.

The eighteenth century has been called "The Age of Enlightenment." It was a period of rapid advance in print culture and publishing, in world exploration, and in the rapid growth of science and technology – all of which had a profound impact on the political and cultural landscape. At the end of the century the American Revolution, French Revolution and Industrial Revolution, perhaps three of the most significant events in modern history, set in motion developments that eventually dominated world political, economic, and social life.

In a groundbreaking effort, Gale initiated a revolution of its own: digitization of epic proportions to preserve these invaluable works in the largest online archive of its kind. Contributions from major world libraries constitute over 175,000 original printed works. Scanned images of the actual pages, rather than transcriptions, recreate the works *as they first appeared.*

Now for the first time, these high-quality digital scans of original works are available via print-on-demand, making them readily accessible to libraries, students, independent scholars, and readers of all ages.

For our initial release we have created seven robust collections to form one the world's most comprehensive catalogs of 18th century works.

Initial Gale ECCO Print Editions collections include:

History and Geography
Rich in titles on English life and social history, this collection spans the world as it was known to eighteenth-century historians and explorers. Titles include a wealth of travel accounts and diaries, histories of nations from throughout the world, and maps and charts of a world that was still being discovered. Students of the War of American Independence will find fascinating accounts from the British side of conflict.

Social Science

Delve into what it was like to live during the eighteenth century by reading the first-hand accounts of everyday people, including city dwellers and farmers, businessmen and bankers, artisans and merchants, artists and their patrons, politicians and their constituents. Original texts make the American, French, and Industrial revolutions vividly contemporary.

Medicine, Science and Technology

Medical theory and practice of the 1700s developed rapidly, as is evidenced by the extensive collection, which includes descriptions of diseases, their conditions, and treatments. Books on science and technology, agriculture, military technology, natural philosophy, even cookbooks, are all contained here.

Literature and Language

Western literary study flows out of eighteenth-century works by Alexander Pope, Daniel Defoe, Henry Fielding, Frances Burney, Denis Diderot, Johann Gottfried Herder, Johann Wolfgang von Goethe, and others. Experience the birth of the modern novel, or compare the development of language using dictionaries and grammar discourses.

Religion and Philosophy

The Age of Enlightenment profoundly enriched religious and philosophical understanding and continues to influence present-day thinking. Works collected here include masterpieces by David Hume, Immanuel Kant, and Jean-Jacques Rousseau, as well as religious sermons and moral debates on the issues of the day, such as the slave trade. The Age of Reason saw conflict between Protestantism and Catholicism transformed into one between faith and logic -- a debate that continues in the twenty-first century.

Law and Reference

This collection reveals the history of English common law and Empire law in a vastly changing world of British expansion. Dominating the legal field is the *Commentaries of the Law of England* by Sir William Blackstone, which first appeared in 1765. Reference works such as almanacs and catalogues continue to educate us by revealing the day-to-day workings of society.

Fine Arts

The eighteenth-century fascination with Greek and Roman antiquity followed the systematic excavation of the ruins at Pompeii and Herculaneum in southern Italy; and after 1750 a neoclassical style dominated all artistic fields. The titles here trace developments in mostly English-language works on painting, sculpture, architecture, music, theater, and other disciplines. Instructional works on musical instruments, catalogs of art objects, comic operas, and more are also included.

old books. new life.

The BiblioLife Network

This project was made possible in part by the BiblioLife Network (BLN), a project aimed at addressing some of the huge challenges facing book preservationists around the world. The BLN includes libraries, library networks, archives, subject matter experts, online communities and library service providers. We believe every book ever published should be available as a high-quality print reproduction; printed on-demand anywhere in the world. This insures the ongoing accessibility of the content and helps generate sustainable revenue for the libraries and organizations that work to preserve these important materials.

The following book is in the "public domain" and represents an authentic reproduction of the text as printed by the original publisher. While we have attempted to accurately maintain the integrity of the original work, there are sometimes problems with the original work or the micro-film from which the books were digitized. This can result in minor errors in reproduction. Possible imperfections include missing and blurred pages, poor pictures, markings and other reproduction issues beyond our control. Because this work is culturally important, we have made it available as part of our commitment to protecting, preserving, and promoting the world's literature.

GUIDE TO FOLD-OUTS MAPS and OVERSIZED IMAGES

The book you are reading was digitized from microfilm captured over the past thirty to forty years. Years after the creation of the original microfilm, the book was converted to digital files and made available in an online database.

In an online database, page images do not need to conform to the size restrictions found in a printed book. When converting these images back into a printed bound book, the page sizes are standardized in ways that maintain the detail of the original. For large images, such as fold-out maps, the original page image is split into two or more pages

Guidelines used to determine how to split the page image follows:

• Some images are split vertically; large images require vertical and horizontal splits.
• For horizontal splits, the content is split left to right.
• For vertical splits, the content is split from top to bottom.
• For both vertical and horizontal splits, the image is processed from top left to bottom right.

THE

DOG-TAX,

A POEM.

BY EDWARD NAIRNE,

OF SANDWICH, IN KENT

INCLUDING

A HINT TO THE MINISTER FOR THE RELIEF OF DOGS,

AND THE

IMPROVEMENT OF THE REVENUE

CANTERBURY

PRINTED FOR THE AUTHOR, BY SIMMONS AND KIRKBY,
AND SOLD BY J JOHNSON, ST PAULS CHURCH YARD, LONDON,
MDCCXCVII
Price Two Shillings and Sixpence.

ERRATA.

Page 7, line 12, *for* therefore *read* thentofore

—— 9, —— 3, *for* hake *read* shake

—— 13, —— 11, *for* dependent *read* dependant

—— 21, —— 18, *for* cae *read* cafe

—— 23, —— 2, *dele* an o *in* too

—— 2,, —— 10, *for* for *read* in

—— 32, —— 1, *for* exhalted *read* exalted

—— 37, —— 5, *for* could I oh, *read* oh, could I

THE DOG-TAX.

INVOCATION.

DOGS and their wrongs, the threat'ning gun and string,
The Tax, and man's ingratitude I sing.

But to thy vot'ry should'st thou, comic muse,
Thy pow'rful aid, which I invoke, refuse,
And leave me (thus deserted) in the lurch,
To smart beneath the critic's pickled birch,
Whipt into madness, as I twist and twine,
'Tis ten to one but that I curse all nine !
Then, (wer't for no cause else,) thou frolic maid,
Lend, for thy sister's sakes, the wish'd for aid,
Let not the oath of phrenzy reach their ear,
I know they will not like to hear me swear.

Would money buy thy favors ? ,as I live,
I have no money,——or I'd freely give,

Nor grudge the Tax to pay, but my small prog

Will not afford it—so I keep no dog;

Nor e'en a cat to watch the fur-clad train,

Who hunt my shelves, but chiefly hunt in vain.

Oft'times I hear their little shrilly cries,

Whilst Fancy paints upon their tiny eyes

The silver tears minute, the pearly beads

Of minikins the little shining heads;

And Fancy tells, too, that each half-starv'd mouse

Threatens to run away and leave my house.

Well! if their little wills determine so,

I'll not oppose—they've my consent to go.

I knew an ancient lady who had pigs!

Reader, if thou art not an ass,

Thou'lt let the solecism pass;

I did not mean that the said lady bore 'em;

Tho' heretofore,

A wicked wh---e,

Of Godalming, they swear,

Did rabbits, very many rabbits bear;

A most abominable indecorum '—

       - Mary Tofts   Our

Our lady had no notion of such rigs ;

Her pigs, for profit, were at market bought,

For she—(God bless her brain-pan) really thought

That pigs, and fowls, and such like elves,

Could get a living, merely of themselves ;

      But, by degrees,

         No beans !

         No peas !

      Her pigs grew scant,

      From right down want ;

And, as they stagger'd in their zig-zag way,

She, quite delighted, frequently would say,

Thinking of course that staggering was prancing,

The merry rogues ! how fond they are of dancing !

  So when a shrivell'd starvling old ram puss ;

Whose painted drap'ry on his bones hung loose,

Look'd in, with unavailing *mew*, and craving

For a small scrap, perhaps not worth the saving,

Tom, Tom, says she unto the quondam prig,

Poor Tom–the taylor's made thy coat too big!

                Oh!

Oh' why did not a certain chapel hold

Three hundred dogmatists, of just such mould,

Who of themselves, uncall'd, so strongly brain'd,

Could go in-doors for shelter when it rain'd,

Or what's still more, in intricacy's spite,

Could count five farthings twice together right;

These were the sort, and on their heads I'd lay

That ev'ry dog would then have had his day.

    Yet, still there's hope, since, in the present set,

(Chosen by patriots, and replete with wit)

Dogs ye have friends, and to your barking saints

Pray for redress of ev'ry dog's complaints.

    But slow and sure is best, more haste, less speed,

Periculous the ground on which they tread;

For oft' a question may be stated so

Much to embarrass Messrs. Aye and No,

And explanations frequently conduce

To make a puzzled matter more abstruse;

Whilst a bad bill is, by amendment's curse,

Instead of better made a d---'nd deal worse——

                          Then

Then, senators, I'd have ye weigh
With caution, ev'ry word ye say,
Nor trust yourselves with even No or Aye;
Be circumspect, it very much behoves,
Be wise as serpents, ye're already *doves*;
Then this, and only this, be pleas'd to say,
We're for the dogs,—the dogs, poor dogs, shant pay.

But hark, the word is pass'd, To horse—to horse—
Clear, clear, stand back, stand back there, clear the course!
Groom, lead out Pegasus the while I strip,
Bring my persuaders*, and my wire-laid whip—

Now, ladies, to the starting-post I'm come,
And wait the signal of the rattling drum;
Bid Peg be gentle, or who chooses
May be rough-rider to the muses.

What's that I hear, odds offered, ten to one!
I'll take that bet, however—Done, sir—done—
Again, sir, if you please—no—I've enough—
Clear—clear—look to—drum flourishes—I'm off—

* Spurs.

POEM.

POEM.

WHEN busy rumour, with his million tongues,
Sustain'd by brazen, or by leathern lungs,
Had forc'd a passage thro' each canine ear, ·
And fill'd dogs noddles with Taxation fear :
When ruthless ministers, with mortal hate,
(Pleading the dire necessities of state),
Would tax all dogs, to raise a large supply,
And those unpaid for should be doom'd to die,
From the young, piddle-drizzling puppy—all [1]
To those great dogs who water at the wall .
Confusion spread thro' ev'ry place,
And, seizing all the canine race,
Sped the fell poison thro' their veins,
Till cordophobia vext their brains :
Urg'd by their wrongs, to madness stung,
The foam fast gath'ring on each tongue,
The shop-dog, house-dog, pedlar, hound,
Each from his prison-house broke ground,

And

And, as Mad Tom* has finely said,

Dogs leapt the hatch, and all were fled.

  Could we have view'd their various tracks,

Cross'd and recross'd on diff'rent tacks,

The traverses they shap'd on land,

Zig-zagg'd by some spasmodic hand,

The diagram had brought to view,

More angles far than Euclid knew.

  But who are competent to keep the logs,

Or mark the Trig-onometry of dogs?

  Now the wild paroxysm o'er,

And dogs grown cool as theretofore,

Instinct points out the proper plan,

And dogs to dogs of wisdom ran,

Imploring them, at once, to meet,

And choose a head, the moſt discreet,

For, malgre! what Tom Pain hath said,

A body's nought without a head.

To Pompey, dog of high renown, .

Well known thro' country and thro' town,

* Vide Lear

Of higher parentage and fame

Than many are, whom I could name,

Speed they—A willing ear he lent,

Advis'd that chosen dogs be sent,

From London, Surry, Sussex, Kent,

And town of Berwick upon Tweed,

And Taffy, knight of the green weed,

Must let hur's tog come up, inteed.

But where could they in safety meet ?

Not in the highway, or the street—

So Wisdom comes, and Pompey jogs,

Gives him the watch-word,—Isle of Dogs.

Th' election o'er, without delay

Unto this Isle they speed their way ;

But note,

The representatives came not to vote

As their constituents pleas'd—a narrow mode ;—

But *pro re nata*—for the gen'ral good.

And now old Thames's waters they divide,

And thro' the rippling waves at pleasure glide ;

Then

Then landing safely on the destin'd shore,

Where few fuch dogs had ever been before,

Halting, they hake their saturated sides,

And raise an atmosphere about their hides.

Next seek they a recess, for they had fears

Of man's impertinence of eyes and ears;

Yet not of ours, since we were never prone

To seek for marrow in *Contention's* bone.

Now acclamations rend the air,

And Pompey's called to the chair!

    Reader, we've seen, on NOMINATION day,

Men of great *promise* and of *high* renown

Driving, like Jehu, to a county town,

And thro' the crowd direct their rapid way;

Then, springing from a curricle, alert,

Leap up into a waggon or a cart,

And looking, with complacent smiles, around,

Make to their MAJESTIES their bows profound!

What! to their Majesties the *King* and *Queen!*

No, no,—the *People's Majesty* I mean;

Which

Which now increased to a *monstrous* heap,

Will soon, (or I mistake,) become dog-cheap—

The simile I mean holds good in part*,

For Pompey likewise leapt into a cart.

   'Twas but a little metaphoric air

We gave ourselves, to call a CART, a CHAIR;

Tho' *dogs* can tell ye, if they choose to speak,

CART, CHAIR, WAIN, WAGGON, are the fame in G*reek*.

With graceful mein o'er the WAIN's front he bends,

And draws the deep attention of his friends.

   Now hear the President, with modest air,

And language chaste, and suitable, declare,

Of great abilities he could not boast,

'Twas on *integrity* he reckon'd most,

And that they might, with confidence, depend

On all his efforts to obtain their end;

Demands their sentiments, then rais'd his paw,

And pointed it to one well vers'd in law,

Who took the hint, tho' he was rather loth

Whithout fome *weighty* reasons to stand forth,

---

* Non omne simile quatuor pedibus currit

HARESKIN

HARESKIN his name, perhaps too fond of praise,

And thus his great forinsic pow'rs displays.

MY DAG*! with all due def'rence and respect

Unto your DAGSHIP, I shall now reflect,

With great asperity, upon a law,

Whose operation, should I find no flaw,

May subject harmless dogs to lose their breath,

By poison, lead, or perpendic'lar death!

I find, my DAG, this act of parliament,

Made at the instigation of one DENT,

Is bas'd in malice, and in guiltlefs.blood,

Ergo, the superstructure can't be good;

And therefore I most strongly do insist

The statute we may legally resist:

Nay, I will be the first to lift my paw

Against this unjust *ex post facto* law;

For I'm a *Hardy* dog; let any man

Make this constructive treason, if he can——

* We are indebted to the Bar for this refined and elegant mode of pronunciation, the familiarity of which in addressing a Judge by the appellation of " My Lad," is peculiarly striking and beautiful.

But

But now concerning *b---s*, for the act

Is silent, I perceive, in that respect;

Not a word mentioned of the female sex;

Of consequence no object of the tax.

> And this is law, I will maintain
>
> Until my dying day, sir,
>
> That *b---s* longer shall remain
>
> Exempted from all pay, sir.

The cheering speech drew wonderful applause

To this expounder of the penal laws.

Next rose a DOG OF GENIUS, CARLO KHAN,

Who, in pathetic language, thus began.

Shall we, of race anterior to the flood,

Tenants of forests and the shelt'ring wood,

Where fragrant violets and lillies blow,

And trees of liberty spontaneous grow,

Shall we, of yore by Providence design'd

To range the wilds and mountains unconfin'd,

Digress into the meads, devoid of fear,

Brave, but innoxious, and as free as air?

* The word b - h does not occur in the act.

Shall

Shall we, rejecting Nature's lib'ral plan,

Crouch, and remain subservient unto man?

Perish the thought, and all who, lost to shame,

Can thus dishonour freedom's facred name!

Hear and believe me, dogs, for now I swear

By those fond doggesses I hold most dear,

Rather than this destruction shall prevail,

I will myself oppose it, *tooth* and *nail*;

And, if I swerve, may ev'ry ill betide

That can humiliate my wonted pride;

May each long, gracefully dependent ear,

Which ev'ry dog of sense is proud to wear,

Roll into ample cylinders, and spread

A foppish ornament around my head,

And may I hear each puppy's jests and rubs,

" Twig Carlo's side curls—smoke the Jack of Clubs"—

Then, with a scarlet spencer on my breast,

Become the subject of eternal jest.

And lastly be—this thought my bosom stings,

Lasht into *allmande steps*, and *ups for kings!*

----

* A German dance.

Hot

Hot and fatigu'd, awhile his head he hung,
And wip'd the slaver from his lolling tongue.

The circumstance, just like a passing cloud,
Obscur'd the speaker from th'applauding crowd:
Thus boys at play, conceal themselves from sight
At hide-fox, till the *Fox* is brought to light.

To other scenes now let us stray awhile
And try some fleeting minutes to beguile,

  Folly to me will often say,

  Why dost not wear a spencer, pray?

  To this I constantly reply,

  A spencer! No, by gad, not I;

The spurious coalition I disdain;

  Rather, much rather, would I meet

  Rude Boreas and his driving sleet,

Endure the cold or face the pelting rain.
What is this starve rump thing! can any say?
And how into the world it made its way?
Is't not a bung'ling taylor's after-thought?
Superfœtation, on a full form'd coat?

But, if this odious fashion must prevail,
And fops will wear their garments in detail,   Let

Let its complexion, jackadandies, show
Some fam'ly semblance of the skirts below——

A son of glorious Mars, one hapless day,
To back of Portsmouth Point did bend his way;
A flashy petit maitre, of some note,
With a strip'd spencer on a scarlet coat;
Quite unsuspicious of a civil war,
Soon as discover'd by the Cyprian corps,
Miss Blainey, for the rights of women, strong,
Calls forth her nereids and heads the throng,
Pours a broadside of rhet'ric at the ape
Who comes in such a questionable shape,
Then, in *chaste* language and the true *sublime*
Names the gross epithet of foreign crime;
And, to a pitch wound up—crop him, she cries—
And swears a pray'r, including both his eyes.

Now warm libations greet his lace,
Jack whips a quid into his face,
His skirts cut off, his spencer torn,
Call'd odious names, in veriest scorn,

Snapt

Snapt short his sword and tippy stick,

And breech dishonored by a kick !

Genius of fashion ! shield thy son—

What must he do ?—Why cut and run—

   Now ending thus our short but boist'rous cruize,

In time call'd in, by signal from the muse,

We'll leave the beau to knot, and splice, and then

We'll sing of dogs, 'till dogs shall talk like men—

   Next rose a HOUSE DOG, who could glibly prate,

Fluent in words, and artful in debate ;

His name, I'll recollect it if I can, sir,

Oh, Sherry-derry-dirry-diddle-dan, sir.

Could shift the scene or subject in a trice,

To India, contracts, bullocks, rack or rice,

Knew much of Hindostan, *(from reading* Dow)

Bob Arcot, Ragaboy, and Purs'ram Bhow ;

But once, to cynic temper giving way,

Detain'd an Asiatic dog, at bay,

During nine years, and dragg'd him thro' the house,

And with his *money baggums* play'd the deuce ;

Better

Better he'd kept (averse to such a scent)

His virulence as well as wit for DENT.

   Now, having ftigmatiz'd the murd'rous plan,

Hear his keen ftrictures upon haughty man.

   In what, I pray, consists man's mighty worth?

He cannot boaft priority of birth;

For God Almighty made great whales, and fprats,

And fhags, and cormorants, and owls, and bats,

And bunting crows, and hogs, and dogs, and cats,

Long before Adam was—and then his brood

Is very little mended fince the flood:

E'en, in my judgment, ministers of kings,

(*Except* DUNDAS and PITT) are no great things.

   Then, seeing we have little chance

But from regen'rate dogs of France,

Or Denmark's dogs, of whom a band

Oft deign'd to visit this our land,

We must on these last dogs rely,

And get redress, or bravely die.

D

I like

I like these dogs, their house*, and farm†,

Because they are so *very* warm;

They'll strive to get repeal'd this cruel law,

By energy of speech or force of paw;

Speak Sheffield daggers to St. Stephen's crew,

Nor cease to badger them 'till all is *blue*.

   Some prais'd his oratory, some, more sage,

Conceiv'd it border'd on intemp'rate rage.

Said, EROSTRATUS, to transmit a name,

The TEMPLE OF DIANA set in flame.

   Now, the great leaders being done,

Some desultory dogs went on,

And talk'd of liberty, and reason's age,

And wisdom, drawn from *Gallia's* page;

Which bringing up a dog of spunk,

Of true BULL breed, nor mad, nor drunk,

He growl'd, " should any on me trench,"

And try to make me read *in French*,

By *George* ! I'd jabber out, " ma foi"

" Je ne lis pas"— " excuzes moi "

* Copenhagen.   † Chalk Farm.

                                        " *Pon*

" *Pon Honour*, do not read to day,

For I'm engag'd *another way*,

And, truth to tell, I'd rather look,

Dogs ear'd or not, in my own Book.

Then rose another, who declar'd

What Pitt deserv'd, for *his* reward,

And said (what ev'ry dog might hear)

Something most cursedly severe.

Laſt rose a dog with chain and plog,

And making, 'tis no joke,

Apostrophe to liberty,

In blubb'ring accents spoke.

O! sticks, and stones,

Brickbats, and bones!

Is liberty then dead?

Or does ſhe nap

In her red cap,

Or from the land is fled?

Another cried——

Your tears be dried,

No

No longer weep nor wail,

    For liberty is now a *Wake* *,

Confin'd in Glostei jail!

    What must she do?

    What courfe puifue?

Her freedom to regain?

    Abide the Law,

    Till its loos'd paw

Shall let her out again.

But seeing, as is oft its fate,

The multitudinous debate,

From oider, as it fiist arose,

Likely to teiminate in blows,

And judging that it might be best

To dedicate an hour to rest;

Now, dogs, says Pompey, ye may ftand at ease,

Roll in the duft, or piddle, if ye please;

Seek bioad emetic grass, oi watei lap,

And I'll lie down and take a little nap.

* kid Wake

TIME, as in times of heretofore

Counts SIXTY MINUTES to the HOUR,

And will not, for impatient man,

Move a jot faster than he can,

Therefore its down and twirl your thumbs,

'Ill tell you when—Oh, here he comes!

   And see the president arise,

And shake his ears, and rub his eyes,

And hear him, on his hinder feet,

With eloquence, th' assembly greet!

Brethren, in jeopardy; I've mark'd your zeal,

And glorious ardor, for the common weal,

Have noted well your sentiments and plan,

T'oppose the base ingratitude of man :

That cruel tyrant, who no kindness shows,

Repays our services with kicks and blows,

Rejects our fond officiousness to please,

And looks us into nothingness with eae :

E'en thus repuest, solicitous, we try

To catch a beam benignant from his eye,

Then

Then, with our tail address this mighty lord,
And beat a parley on the sounding board!
Should these our overtures by chance succeed,
(A condescension wonderful indeed!)
Eager, we spring to shew the pleasing trick,
Play with his glove, his handkerchief, or stick;
Dash in the water at his first command,
And bring his venture unimpair'd to land—
Nor does one surly dog, or crabbed cur,
To his capricio's make the least demur,
Save, when curft avarice denies the boon,
To him all dark admidst the blaze of noon,
Or, when pale famish'd suppliants implore,
Unwillingly we chase them from the door.

Amid the howlings of the winter's wind,
Guilt fear'd the night, but more he fear'd mankind;
Heard his strong bars, in fancy, burst in twain,
Saw rapine, and saw murder in his train,
Saw him, terrific, shake his bloody crest,
And felt the dagger at his throbbing breast;

Palsied

Palsied with horror and with dread dismay,

Trembling he shrunk and fear'd too look for day,

But hark, to save untouch'd, a useless hoard,

His faithful dog he'd destin'd to the cord!

How wide the contrast from the gen'ious soul,

Who fears nor poinards nor the poison'd bowl;

Lib'ral and tender to the dog he keeps,

Lives free from dread, and safe from danger sleeps.

Yet, here, let justice candidly declare,

That many thousands, 'mongst mankind, there are,

In whose expanded minds the virtues glow,

And, feeling, can relieve another's woe.

Should ought of gall proceed from satire's pen,

Apply it only to the worst of men——

How much is mystic science, by our lore,

Rescu'd from errors of the days of yore!

E'en GALILEO might have died a fool,

But for the lessons of our dancing school.

Would NEWTON or COPERNICUS have known

The planets revolution round the sun,

But

But by attending to the active feats

Of dogs that dance round Brum in the streets?

 See *(near the centre plac'd)* the Great Bear roll

In solemn saraband, around his pole!

And dogs, in sprightlier measures, trip it round,

And print their orbits on the yielding ground;

Whilst hurdy-gurdy tones delight the ears,

And represent the music of the spheres.

 But now we'll speak, (with such grand things in truce)

Of food, and raiment, elegance and use—

 How many dogs deceased, some of note,

Which daily on old Thames' waters float,

Seized with avidity, and taken home,

Chopt fine, and season'd, sausages become!

Whilst epicures new dainties still create,

And *puppies* drown that *house-lamb* may be fat,

For doggess' milk, deny it if you choose,

Is more nutritious than the milk of ewes—

 How does the soft, cosmetic, dogskin glove,

The arm of beauty whiten and improve,

How

How many efflorescences give place,

Lick'd by Narcissus' tongue, from beauty's face,

Whilst, for his meed, superlatively blest,

His feet soft patting on her snowy breast,

He seeks her eyes, and then, extatic, sips

Cœlestial nectar from Maria's lips ;

Whilst beaux, refus'd this exquisite delight,

Plung'd in despair, grow frantic at the sight.

The sons of Galen frequently impart

A grand specific for the curing art ;

Its name, 'mongst med'cines for the gout and p-x,

Shines in large letters on the painted box,

Should any doubt its powers, let him pop

His nose into a pothecary's shop,

He'll find that *album græcum* can dispense

Its fragrant odours strong as frankincense.

And yet mankind will wage th'unequal strife

With dogs and doggesses, from early life !

Scarce has Lucina's kind, obstetric aid,

Our hapless offspring to the world convey'd,

Ere the uneven scales decide their fate,

As whim, or prejudice put in the weight,

The harmless whelps, weak, rickety, and blind,

Snatch'd from the litter, and to death consign'd,

Are hurl'd in rivers, ditches, ponds, or pools,

The spoit of wanton boys and upgrown fools,

And, ere the mercy of the yielding wave

Admits the victims to their wat'ry grave,

Bruis'd are their with'ring bodies, crush'd their bones,

By urchin boys, with *missile* clods and stones ;

Whilst men, whom acts of savageness delight,

Applaud, and dwell, with pleasure, on the sight :

But mark of evil cruelty's a root,

The gallows, not unfrequently, the fruit;

Then check this vice, or, miscreants, ye may see

Your darlings dangle on the fatal tree.

At what has mankind taken such offence ?

Is fear of running mad, the weak pretence ?

Parturient doggesses, in straw confin'd—

Dreading the wat'ry exit of their kind,

Whi!

While they anticipate the direful scenes,

Know ye that HYDROPHOBIA supervenes!

Should harm result, let man, whate'er th' amount,

In juſtice place it to his own account.

E'en now 'tis thought, that waterdreading Pitt,

And Hal Dundas, have terribly been bit:

For, 'tis notorious, they have lately run

Their heads, with all their might, against a tun,

Have saddled horses, stampt the people's hats,

And soon will go a hunting after cats!

When ministers to madness are inclin'd,

Really 'tis proper they ſhould be confin'd—

And man, too, must beware, for, sure as fate,

More mischief's now impending o'er his pate:

" On * mules and dogs th' infection first began,

" And last the vengeful arrows fix'd in man."

Then wear your *hats*, to guard your *polls*, and dread

The twinking blister ready for your head.

Blessed are those who have not lent

Their ears to Pitt, Dundas, or Dent;

* Iliad, book I

E 2   For

For should they, *by their merits*, rise

Some twenty feet towards the skies,

And probable it is that some,

PAVEMENT SURVEYORS MAY BECOME,

They'd want,—so high their exaltation!

Those ears to hold them in their station.

    Brethren, with much concern, I understand

A mania rages in a neighb'ring land,

'Tis self induc'd—than hydrophobia worse,

And these sad dogs must be repell'd with force,

For nought can check the dangerous complaint,

But copious bleeding and severe restraint—

Legions of these distracted gallic dogs,

With wildest fury tearing off their plogs!

Have run thro' Savoy, Italy, and Spain,

Torn the Pope's bulls, and turn'd the Don dogs' brain,

Attack'd our friends, who justly have withstood,

And delug'd Austria with her noblest blood;

Yet once she reckon'd on a potent friend,

A heroine, dwelling at the world's north end,

Where

Where *Ursa Major* with *Arcturus* glow,

And gild the regions of eternal snow:

Her sceptre was a pole, with outstretcht hand,

She wav'd it o'er unmeasured tracts of land,

And to this magic pole's extended sway,

Miriads of lesser poles did then give way!

Meant she to call her hardy legions forth?

This *bow-wow-wowsky* of the blust'ring north?

 Oh! may the successor of bouncing Kate,

(Just like a white louse on a school-boy's slate)

Confine a certain *mercenary dog*,

(Lur'd by a heap of stolen˙, royal prog)

And with his finger circumscribe his bounds,

Till, slaughter'd *like Actæon*, by his hounds,

Or treated with the rigour he deserves,

He keeps him pris'ner till he drowns or starves.

 When mischief threats, such sad dogs, looking on,

Are worse than mad dogs, twenty times to one——

˙ Supposed to be certain jewels late belonging to Louis the XVIth and his Queen

To

The dogs of Holland, too, have had their fits,

Why Hogen Mogen must have lost his *wits*,

To *court* the danger, run into the way,

And thus become a voluntary prey !—

He's justly serv'd, and, on my soul, I'm glad

To see *Van Pug* so fraterniz'd and mad—

But some alarmists say, these dogs of France

Have at Great Britain lately look'd askance ;

Were there no bounds to check their wild career,

'Tis likely they might think of coming here,

But dread the water, and a dog nam'd *Howe*,

A dauntless one, and Britain's big bow-wow—

Whose flaming throats, and rows of iron teeth,

Thousands of French dogs have consign'd to death.

But *should* these boasters of their *freedom* come,

Forc'd by their tyrants from their native home,

Perchance they'll hear the British Lion roar

A little louder than he's done before ;

Whilst our stanch bull-dogs, faithful to their trust,

Retort their phrase, and make *them—bite the dust*

* John de Wit was a famous Dutch Statesman, he, and his brother Cornelius, were assassinated by the populace at the Hague, in 1674

But,

But, now, the subject matter we'll resume,

And, leaving Spain and Holland to their doom,

Detesting all such renegado elves,

We speak of worthier dogs—we mean ourselves;

Since men there are who, almost from our birth,

Protect, and well appreciate our worth;

Do not the most discerning of mankind,

(Those not to prejudice or error blind)

Consign our race to enviable fame,

And sanction us with some illustrious name?

Gods, demi-gods, and *poets*, emp'rors, kings,

Heroes, of whom the bard sublimely sings,

Achilles, Hector, Memnon, too, he cries,

Nestor persuasive, and Ulysses wise,

Ajax and Diomed, unmov'd by fear,

And Merion, dreadful as the God of War?

  Or do our females, beautiful and fair,

Of appellation lose their rightful share?

No—Pallas, Dian, Hebe, Flora prove,

Psyche, and Venus, whom I dearly love;

                   And

And some. exhalted to eternal fame,

Bear of high heav'ns imperial Queen the name.

 When Jove, immortal Jove, had got the *Itch*

Or rather *knack* of calling Juno, b---h,

The thund'rer most undoubtedly did mean

Some trif'ling degradation to his Queen ;

But the comparifon will clearly prove

To whom the compliment was meant from Jove,

For what the one, no room for doubt remains,

Loses in eminence, the other gains.

 Thus, when Apollo, fervid God of Day,

Obliquely on a mirror darts his ray,

Th' illumin'd object or opticians lie

Reflective sends his image to the sky ,

Our females were the mirrors, so says fame,

On which the mighty Jove imping'd her name,

And which, with little diminution, they

Return'd to Heav'n again without delay,

By Jove" compar'd, it is a number given,

A b---h on earth, is like a b---h in Heav'n ;

~ Sic sitae laetantur ——

But

But now, whilst time allows me ample room,

The great, th' important subject I'll resume:

Friends, neighbours, relatives or whatsoe'er

Title or appellation ye may bear,

Whether thro' China orbs ye drink the light

Or only boast a moiety of sight,

Swivel or wall-eye, *sine* left or right;

Whether your bodies crooked be or straight,

Whether ye hitch or shamble in your gait;

Or whether hound, or blood-hound, mastiff, tike,

Turnspit or terrier, ye're to me alike.

I shall address you, since you've equal caim,

By a more gen'raland endearing name;

Then, with a voice at once profound and clear,

Silence, he cried, *ye sons of bitches hear!*

Hear me with candour, patiently attend,

And freely censure what ye can't commend:

I've mark'd, as I have said before, your zeal

And glorious ardor for the common weal,

Have

Have noted well your sentiments and plan

T'oppose the base ingratitude of man;

With you I reprobate their cruel laws,

Yet much I dread the *energy* of *paws*.

How can we wage with them th' unequal strife,

Fraught with such peril to our limb and life?

Or how be justified, in times like these,

To propagate our race, mankind to please;

No, from such intercourse we must abstain,

'Till pestilence shall spread, and vermin reign;

Yet let us not, in terms abrupt, declare,

This our intention, to the grieving fair,

Lest some reproachfully deride, and some,

Of weaker nerves, alarmists should become;

But softly tell them chastity sublimes,

And bid them hope more favourable times,

For come they must, when we shall, void of fear,

Solace and hold them more than ever dear.

Now when our species shall be hang'd or die,

And man, depriv'd of dogs the flesh supply,

Then

Then putrid offal shall defile the ground,

And pestilence and famine stalk around;

Whilst at the *quondam* dog-protected farm,

Vermin of all denominations swarm;

And mice and rats, become a dauntless race,

Mount on his board and stare him in the face,

Nor shall one dog molest a daring rat,

Or modern Whittington, supply a cat;

Then shall he threat, and grievously complain,

And threat he may, but he shall threat in vain.

One man unto the limpid river's brink

May lead a horse, but can he make him drink?

Not if he sai-yeth *neigh*—nor nineteen more

Can urge him, 'gainst his negative, from shore;

Mount him and ride him in, 'twould be in vain,

'Twere better, friend, thou rids't him out again.

A horse, in this respect, is like a king,

For should two orders of the *tiers etat*,*

A bill in parliament contrive to draw;

* Pronounced, *etau.*

Or

Or of St Stephen's beast should make a hack,

And clap a lordly rider on his back.

Le Roi, may say " *S'avisera*"—

That's, in plain English, I'll have no such thing

Still are king's vetos human I opine,

Whilst horses vetos are of right divine;

'Tis so with us, for if we disapprove,

The world in arms can't force us into love.

   Now hear the eulogist of dogs declare,

(Some folks may smile and think me insincere)

By all the implements of mischief, stones,

Tin canisters and lanterns, kettles, bones,

Turnips or tiles, with which mankind assail,

Drive at their heads, or fasten to their tail:

The lantern-tying system I detest,

And 'gainst it mean to enter my protest;

For nothing done to dogs I really deem

So much degrades them in their own esteem.

Were I a lurcher, but it can't be so,

D—mme, young gentlemen, I'd let ye know

* The expreffion (in Norman French) made ufe of to declare a refufal of the royal affent to bills in parliament

What

What 'tis to worry dogs—I would not baik,

But slyly watch your waters in the dark ;

Give your high bipednesses such a greet,

Nor quit my hold till all my grinders met.

    Could I oh, hold at Peter's* vivid fire,

To warm, but not to burn, my frigid lyre,

His, who can roaft nobility by shoals,

And diaw his Grace of Richmond *o'er the coals* ;

Then would I shine, and sweetly touch each string,

And thus to Sirius† would I say or sing :

    O rag'ing, thou, whose all distressing heat,

Can put the sons of men into a sweat ;

Thou who iejoiceth in their sighs and groans,

And hold'st dominion e'er their brittle bones.

When thou the circuit of the skies shalt run,

(*Associate to the* LORD CHIEF JUSTICE SUN)

If e'ei I view'd thee, with supreme delight,

Daiting thy arrows in the awful night ;

Gieat tutelary star, thy shafts employ,

Favour dogs, friends, and all their foes annoy.

---

* Peter Pindai.   † Sirius, oi the Dog ftai, in the Dog-days rifes and fets with the Sun

Punish with accidents, each ape and fool,

Dash them in sloughs or in the mantled pool;

And make them glad on each disastrous day,

To gather up their limbs and hop away.

    Were retribution and reward but mine,

Since Ministers will (duty free) have wine;

Since Champagne *pales* them not, nor gin, makes *blue*

I'll say, in confidence, what I would do—

Give them strong Lisbon, to inflame,

And Port, to keep them red with ſhame;

Fox would have Sherry—Sherry, Foxey get,

But Dent drink verjuice, till it made him sweat.

    But now the shadows of declining day,

Reminding POMP, how time had ſlipt away;

And as they meant *on foot* to travel home,

Directly to the point, says he, I'll come.

    Then, brethren, 'stead of unavailing force,

Or love represt, let's try another course;

And that, 'twixt dogs and men, all strife may cease,

(Ourselves degrading) we will sue for peace.

To

To which, if Ministers shall nod assent,

All shall be pardon'd, but that dog-rogue, *Dent*

Then shall our females, free from dire alarms,

Repose in confidence within our arms.

And, as our race increasea nd multiply,

Shall vermin crews in all directions fly;

Plenty shall smile, men breathe salubrious air,

Dogs their unshaken loyalty declare.

And (what's devoutly to be wish'd) I trow,

The treasury with conscious worth shall glow.

The plan is simple, easy to pursue,

That he who keeps no dog, shall pay for *two*.

But should our voluntary offers fail,

I'll an example set, and take the veil.

No more with Veney will I frisk and play,

In the broad sunshine of the garish day,

Lest her soft blandishments may haplefs move

My warm desires beyond platonic love.

No, I'm resolv'd, nor will I converse hold,

Save with chaste Dian, or Latona cold;

I'll wink at Larcenies, of scaddle cats,

And grant an armistice to mice and rats;

Call polecats, puttices, and weasels, brother,

And d-mn that trait'rous dog who kills another.

 Bowing he made a motion to depart,

But ere 'twas possible to leave the cart,

A sense of gratitude inspir'd all ranks,

The president shall have our genuine thanks;

Such as from dogs were never heard before,

Shall shake the isle and make the welkin roar.

 I'll pass the word, says Cæsar, all agree

To cheer the worthy president with *three*,

Up paws, mark well the signal—now—

Pompey for ever—*Bow-wow-wow*.

F I N I S.

Ingram Content Group UK Ltd.
Milton Keynes UK
UKHW032104100323
418413UK00016B/113